the ice stayed but the water left

the ice stayed but the water left

Poems

Chad Weeden

BROKEN TRIBE PRESS

the ice stayed but the water left

Copyright © 2025 Chad Weeden
First Edition

Paperback ISBN: 978-1-965412-06-0

Library of Congress Control Number: 2025900725

Cover art by Chad Weeden
Author photo by Trenda Boone

Published by Broken Tribe Press
Lawrence Landing Company
Raleigh, North Carolina 27609
USA, North America

Broken Tribe Press is a proud member of:

Independent Book Publishers Association
 and
Community of Literary Magazines and Presses

www.brokentribepress.com

BROKEN TRIBE PRESS

for Trenda

ADVANCE PRAISE

These poems are sharp and glittering, poems about desire, relationships, loss. Chad Weeden's images are powerful, translating emotional states into sirens and flame, fog and stars. There's danger here, and beauty: "Funny how a flailing ripcord/makes us listen to the wind for the first/and last time." This is a gorgeous collection by a wonderful poet.

—Becky Hagenston,
  author of *The Age of Discovery and Other Stories*

Chad Weeden's collection *the ice stayed but the water left* takes unlikely, even ordinary, moments, and infuses them with significance and even beauty. "He hovers above the sink like an old disease," he writes, and "Trash piles up when you're gone wrangling the infinite sea." The poems peel back layers to reveal deep truths— "...why we decorate the crawlspace with tea leaves and relics abandoned of exotic molds we try so hard to fit into we forget what it's like to be destroyed," and "What will burn will burn because it can. Not because it should." He explores the coldest grief and regret—"His one suit hangs on the bedroom door so you can take it to the funeral home," and "I am an echo between two windows," and "I was a burden. You were a chore . . ." Chad is a poet sensitive to nature in all her vicissitudes, sensitive also to sound and image. His poems sometimes whisper, sometimes scream. I'm blown away by the sheer beauty of this collection.

—Lori Baker Martin,
  poetry editor of *The Midwest Quarterly*

Chad Weeden's poems are set in contemporary spaces: people navigating complicated logistics, pivoting from one room to another, reaching for the future while trying to put the past to rest. And yet, these lines transport us to a place of betweenness, a world of fertile bardos, Weeden's speakers navigating the underworld like a contemporary Virgil. Throughout this thrilling debut, a reader is ushered through archetypal domains, realms beyond the one with which we're so familiar. We're reoriented to the epic, the continuum that's always unfolding just beyond our comprehension. This is a book to celebrate, to read and reread.

—John Amen, author of *Dark Souvenirs*,
    editor of *Pedestal Magazine*

The stew that serves as the poetry of Chad Weeden is equal parts science, surrealism, and unyielding biological synchronicity that recognizes the magic in the everyday, and forces the reader to acknowledge their part in the flow. Poetry gives shape and sonic architecture to the unseen elements that comprise our lives, and in line after line, Weeden's poetry serves as a camera illuminating those various aspects and recording them, making tangible "the air in a piano and the inertia in a rented room." NC buys more books of poetry per capita than any other state and this is one collection from an up-and-coming Tarheel artist that I highly recommend you add to your library.

—Keith Flynn, author of *The Skin of Meaning*,
    editor of *Asheville Poetry Review*

A stone upon a path knows
more than I do of the rain.

- Patrick Lane

CONTENTS

///

////

Vantage Point

We outlived the outlines,
prints in concrete, forgotten on the sidewalk,

no thanks to rain or the street sweeper's lust
to erase the half-identified off the curbs

of our paved gardens. Seeds ricochet.
Wind-quivered. As good as gone

when rooted to our faults, the whole block
two loaded steps from ever growing out of it.

November postpartum was chalk
dust and feathers in your windowsill.

I was a burden. You were a chore,
so they said. It was obvious we couldn't help

ourselves unlike the crows hunched on escape
railings, the one that'd leave you keys

and bottle caps, your grandmother's wedding
ring you buried in a flower pot. But who peeled

out before the sirens stalled? We were elevated
without our graffitied parts, a brisk hopscotch

across the chaos intersecting Hound and Brevard.
If we made it, we'd meet at the fire hydrant

between telephone poles stapled with the missing
whose names didn't change the way we moved

to the hum of traffic, again—waiting for street
lights to spark forbidden shortcuts down the alley

where we'd smash a can and chase it through neon
slush, caught in the ivy on the barbed wire beyond

our wilderness, no matter the holes in our shoes,
tangled sweater sleeves. It was a straight shot then,

echoes after that night we surrendered ourselves
to the shape of our breath, when we found a handful

of coins in a dead man's cup and raced like run-
aways across the bridge, to the top of the water tower,

hours past our bedtime,
throwing quarters at the moon.

Knotted Wave

Trash piles up when you're gone
wrangling the infinite sea. Sail-

torn, voodoo shrouds. Double
knots by default. And all at once

you're out of body. You'd rather
chuck the lines than tie them,

like will or won't they hold.
But steady is the tension is the wake

that follows. Look at you, at me,
the gossamer beyond. Anywhere

off course somehow you come
full circle. How do we disappear

from ourselves in watered-down
silence? Maydays' fizzling on a shortwave

once you realize the void is just ahead,
as it was, tarnished, frozen in bare

definition. Everything overboard.
Balloons and cogs, refrigerators

like bouquet mines. I'm slow
to surface if it weren't for galaxy

glimpses at the end of a dead-end street.
Nobody on watch to read the wind.

Buoy bells eroding. I lace the bags
and heave them to the yard, blind

autopilot, a coast clear enough
to see all the boats at the bottom.

Marrow

Every other day, post-dawn on the hour, the bearded
man in camouflage assumes the corner booth, orders
a slice of pie, a coffee he won't drink, and cyclone
spoons a steady dribble down the side, halos on the
table and no one's looking at charcoaled finger prints,
knuckles scabbed like a junkyard car that hasn't
moved since the wheels were white and lifted after a
tree burst through the windshield. If the mug doesn't
sear his hands to touch it isn't hot. And he'll tell you.
It's really the scent he's after, that dream trigger, says
he hasn't had a sip since they banned lead from
gasoline, just needs to have something finite he can
stare into where he forgets his origins, something
warmer than reality he can raise to his lips when
reconsidering a pause he's held longer than the
history of small talk. It's easy to roll your eyes. I have.
Though his trance is contagious. How he studies the
steam to lure its spirals from the fog behind his
glasses. Because what else is there anymore when
desire is not what you think it is other than ripples of
porcelain chatter? So to pull his focus, draw a stool
that doesn't spin. Ask about the inked anaconda from
wrist to ankle. But don't mention the weather or the
flow of his digressions unless you want to be seduced
to the air that life isn't what it used to be—what it
never was. Kindred ties. Streaks of joy like metal in a
microwave. He'll say before the great recede this once
was a lake, where we're sitting now, how he sold the
marrow of his bliss for the creature inside.

Dumbstruck desolation. The stalled engines lumped along the dirt as monuments of his wary devotion to absent machines on the fringe of exile till his voice grinds like a wax recording. Ask him to pass the sugar, or why death doesn't wait anymore in the breezeway for the cook to skillet-pound flesh on the fire as you pry another dollar from the register instead of asking for a refill.

Circuits

After   noon. On a some
day   June in a recovery room.

Move   father. You aren't
stained in glass yet. Run

child. You are not hard-
wired to breakers. They are

only baffled by your circuitries.
The knobs that won't budge

and the shorts in the extension
cords that reveal us all in darkness.

Pinch the fuse and you can still
escape the inkblot's translation,

but don't be afraid of the electric
chair. Say   they're stars,

memoirs   of a skip-tracer.
Or the ghosts of traffic jams

from when you'd bend back
power lines so the recoil

might unplug you.

Bridled

You let it ride. Zeros to etcetera.
All Calypso. Bribed the bookie

with your parlor guitar but Lady
Luck jacks your derby hat either way.

From the bleachers to the starting gate,
we bare our rituals of hazard, our fitted

indentations for every bell-lap like a blunt
uppercut when the bargain fortune teller's

prediction fails. Blame Luna for her opposing
stride or the jockey who purged as the gates

released. *It's a sure thing*, the teller says,
taking off her glasses, *this sprint to the singularity,*

to be has-been satellite specks in the announcer's
binoculars. You dismount the charge, take

whips to your spine for charity and all the
fractured horses destined for carousels.

Bite through the bridle. The mint julep's
are free if you pace yourself to apprehend

the idleness of waiting on waiting,
you're waving your flag at a mechanical bull.

Ground Delays

A van heaped in ladders runs a stop light,
swerves to miss the point and ricochets
down the hillside. You think the fog's gone
since you can see the braids of tire treads
from potholes that rattle us upon arrival.
But it's never quite what's in front—is it.
Hubcaps dam the river. You try to hurry
on by, like a boulder. The fog makes it easy
to curse the muse, to complement her
obscurity, the weight of her distance
like gravel in your chest, how you wring
the rabbit ears wild for stellar transmissions
that could tease a ghost town. We are
wired to short circuit. You better hold on to
something, still you doubt it, the lithium
stashed when she wants to tell you what to say,
your mouth a well, speechless in a strait-
jacket. And as you recede, the imposters shudder
in the idle hours. They talk faster than you
can think. So all you can do is raid the hollows
for her masterpiece, or jog your mind around
the corner, cranes raised, all scraps and lumber,
as far as another story will go from your child-
hood home. But the question begs, why do we
trust these crumbling plates of space, the wing
walkers in the jet streams that strip the scaffolding
that creaks your name, as the tapestry sags with
icicles older than we are. It catches up, eventually,
or it burns out, the ones that split and dive and
pierce the drywall, where you sleep sound in dark
matter, indefinite, light headed from the sky

lights. You were an observatory aimed at the void. Absorbing everything everywhere but the source, which was off limits. Ground delays for days. Power outage in paradise. Then the telescopes collapsed, no radar but your naked eyes to find her center, your foundation sinking from blocks that dropped after put into place.

B-sides

Listen—the amplifiers feedback, porous
drone, what the heart skips in the overwrite.

You were the cough that struck the cadence,
fourth take, erased, then record until warped

and drowsy, like the basement demos I can't
rewind without severing. But I do because

who wouldn't? If only out of boredom
for the impossible nostalgia I mix back

together for exaggerated breaths. And while
I'm familiar with the acoustics of concrete,

the music gets mangled, estranged like cardiac
articulations from a chorus cut short and spliced

to a voicemail of your mom confronting God.
Battery low, inbox full. A threnody to be

continued. I flip sides and fast forward
till the tapes unravel those duets you screamed

with yourself, clear to hoarse to quivering
in a phone booth underneath the marquee

that lost its letters. I'd be scrapped before
the intermission, grainy falsetto and isle-

tripping to the curb I know like a stage
like a cliff where the maestro draws his

podium to the lip and accents the back-
ground noise with a marching band strung

out on echoes and rarities. How many
octaves off? Measures apart. So we

missed the bridge again. Horns full
of water. Our tangled encores, capillaries

from stuck cassettes, used or not, as if
the low fidelity of your stereo tremors

would feed us back into our bodies.

Smoke Stacks

On missed re-entries: state your purpose
then defeat it. Funny how a flailing ripcord

makes us listen to the wind for the first
or last time. Although we want to fall.

Into holes. And there's going to be holes.
But what are we without them? Mired

in shells. Devoured by the static after dusk
that let's us curse the soul of complacent

sadness. Wring it out for the words, the rage
because this is home and home as it will ever

be, this palace, an elaborate sabotage faded
black with fire. But is it smoke or love that stunts

our growth? Loopy when we met, we eloped
on stacks that shaped and spread the clouds,

that changed the color of meteors
from streaks unseen to grenadine horses.

Crevices

Distance is deceiving for the man traveling the scenic
stretch just beyond the valley. It's all familiar from
back there, until up close, personal, like the landscape
of his face, both arid and unrecognizable as the miles
trekked, carved, but wouldn't get attached to the
territory. Even off rails he kept his lane, when gone for
a season more, through speed traps and boom towns
that grew like the gash in his left sole from stepping in
and out of the car, his wrinkled maps draped across
the passenger seat, Appalachia wedged in the door
like the boundary folds of everywhere he roamed. And
peddled. A vacuum from the Buick trunk, or bibles.
After a while he figured it's the cleanest houses that
have something to hide. But those first impressions,
he'd say, when they note your shoes, scuffed or dirty,
Berluti knots untied—that's all they remember. And
no one wants what you think they need if you can't sell
the demonstration.

Despite the dance, he learned to walk away with
nothing but split heels or footprints in the carpet.
There was no rhyme to his return when he'd show up,
road-weary, under quota, sipping something strong
on the driveway, a music box on my pillow. He liked
to blame the shoes and say they lost their luster, so
the night before he'd leave again he'd line them on the
ottoman's edge to separate soles, to renew the finish
of stale leather, the cracks and holes he'd mend with
brush and rag as he rubbed the haze from the oxfords,
three coats—no less, no more relacing backward steps

moving forward. The way he'd outshine his reflection with spit alone to see himself renovated, the pride of a statue, even though most toes cannot be fixed once they're grazed—like slits in velvet socks, the day-to-day smudge shuffling, stumbling dispositions with a nail through his boot, his barefoot other. It's always the closing touch, the final smear of gloss on the loafers, his meridian flow short of excess like the burlap bear tucked over in a drawer.

Lazy eye. Empty polish tins rattling my panoramic squint. My bunk too high, I'd climb down a ladder of dueling bayonets, sleepless walker, a night crawler feeling for crevices, my ear to the floor to a loose board by the closet and meter his wheezing like the comatose drone of the San Andres. You can't buff it all out. Revelations taken for granted. If he heard me listening, he'd plant needle to vinyl as I'd inch toward the sill to the listless metronome of his double-brush, Jean Ritchie humming ballads to the dead where even the purest shade of rapture couldn't lift me.

Understanding Gravity

When a flame fills a jar
the sky deflates like a mattress.
Satellites crown the aura. Orion's
out of arrows and Perseus let go
of his sword. You reascend
like a pulled parachute, thinking
the stars are yours to keep,
the way you puncture clouds
with a bent antenna, poking
the firmament like a dead raccoon.
But radio voices don't believe
in ordinary miracles. And you're
through the roof as usual.
Pale kamikaze. A trail of arrivals
dispatched from a can. It takes a
winter and a thousand collisions
for every one departure, no matter
how predictable the static or the pulse
of your broom sweeping acres of debris
to shroud the runway from your mind.
Ground control: the ice is clear for landing.
All the weather reports disagree. But who
would chance an endless cloud? Chaos
marks the turbulence—nowhere Illinois,
seatbelts unfastened and we're floating
as the pressure drops a bag of oxygen
after you strung wind chimes from
the rafters so when the house shakes
at least it's in harmony. You regret

the tone. But this one stays in your
head, can't hide from the sound now
or the rhythm of dust and fading.
Eventually the tambourine skips a beat,
lost count, and soon the other world
demands us from thin air. In we breathe
the sacred exhaust. Hijacked. Another
nosedive beyond repair. Whatever tilts
yourself after the fact, this is why
we're torn from our bodies, why we
decorate the crawlspace with tea leaves
and relics abandoned of exotic molds
we try so hard to fit into we forget what
it's like to be destroyed.

Tea Leaves

Sagan ladles the cosmos
into the kettle I fail to fill

or refill too high. From splash
to puddle, you have my

attention. This instant. But
I am prone to dozing. And

when injected with stars,
I spill what I boil,

for glints of ecstasy
except to shrink the aperture

of light that lifts you wholly
only to see what's in frame:

our pale dots, a nebula
or scratched negative,

same thing, both lush
with dust and isolated

matter of everything
we thought we had

that wouldn't strain
that couldn't be

revived with water.

Subdivisions

How many hawks above the demolition?
Soot-coated like the moon, circling the stench
of what remains when we divide: Arabella
Bridge, your abyss, a pair of bloodhounds
roped to the welcome sign, hunched
and fevered, ready to charge a right of passage
out of range. They say it's controlled. That it's
dire, life's benign repetition, until it's not.
But so's the course. Like longevity's flawed
arithmetic—if I don't see you here, I'll see
you there, new monotony, on the edge
of Gypsy Park, where we'd sit for an hour
every other Tuesday on a bus stop bench
as the kudzu giants absorbed the subdivision.
I'd arrive early. Disarmed the moment
to scrub the rows of tabloid foliage, sizing
the obituaries for palpitations and a role model
of the atomic age. *I wasn't waving at you*, he'd say,
I was blocking the sun. Eyes glossy and green,
he'd dull the light if it was harsh. Which is why
he was always late, by routine, blank like attic
manuscripts, zippo-flicking through bleary phantasms
of a woman scaling fish on a beach, his brother
yelling from a dune, or the prescriptions forgotten,
always patting his breast pocket for that full rattle
of capsules I doubt he strained his exhalations
on purpose. We'd crouch and cover. Wrapped in vines
like who will cut our passage from the overgrowth
to the cradle that rocks against the tremors enough
to inch our asylum from creases in a milestone.

Vessels

She wore an apron stained like arctic cliffs,
harborless, a legend weathering brittle specks
of jade off her clavicle. Dogwood's blossomed

through a barred garden, transcending a hail-
ladened applause after eras of windswept
fatigue chiseled canyons to induce continental

drift. My orbit was rewritten, polar ends
irretrievable like dim epiphanies on how
to score the sacred curves of alabaster shores

unwashed by her wake. She was born rotating.
Wheel-thrown, interpreting your surface through
pinch and water until she'd excavate fault lines

beyond the tundra of your mind. What you
didn't know about mud and oil, stripped your
braids and ragged palms, made you plead

with portraits etched in caves sealed off by
Providence. I'd repeat my wrongs, rake my
scarlet scraps into voodoo pots and turn them

to hurricane cauldrons. I was a landslide of
gravel organs leveling her galleries, clipping
articles for a kiln brimmed with porcelain bones

like monuments for the missing, exhibit *Untitled*,
just her thumb prints on the belly of a vase.

Jukebox Murmurs

Skinny like a dancer.
Hurl me in your sodden sway,
my arrhythmia, I admit
defeat sooner than the curtain
calls upon our reckless flow, to be as fluid
as you, unfashionably late, tiptoe
migrations from one oblivion
to another. When sepia cracks
its not so easy to hide yourself
among strangers, two steps
between us as you twist the filter
off a Lucky Strike and raise
a candle to your face. History
begins with ash and us repeating
we were always out of time.
      Meanwhile, it's 4am.
A free-for-all in the ballroom.
And you're sleep-starved for polaroid
proof of the best it gets
since Grace robbed your opulence
with her anemic kind of glare.
So you kicked her cane
up off the floor and pressed
ahead where the jukebox
murmurs cosmic ultimatums:
lick the spoon or wipe your eyes
just to say you saw it coming,
the daily disappearances, to
and from, searching for a second

wind that'd sing your sentences,
to wish you nothing but the fear
of some manic forever.
      Yeah, I guess
you had to be there. Disarray
and all, our feigned elegance in the
off chance we'd get it right this once.
But the heart's a guarded chore.
What we purge. We devour. And tag
along like we'd salvage our missteps
from tired choreographies: and again,
five, and six, and seven, eight—trip to touch
a hazy slumber. Twirl yourself into lullaby.

Bread Crumbs

Imagine a river, a bed.
The ice stayed but the water left

us deep blue to forfeit our slings
for rumors of air. Crippled love.

Couldn't hold our X-rays
to the sun. We were malleable

like nightcrawlers on a hook
until the gash in the horizon

flopped us off the moor and dangled
our greedy silhouettes to burn

or sparkle in peroxide froth. What
is it about pain that undresses

the mind from the marrow? We slip
and we fight our heart-to-hearts

in fevered sleep talk, chests swelling
like inhaled whispers as we try to wrap

the gauze enough to feel the contours
without our shadows. Bite marks

in the iodine splatter. And had you
mentioned the hunger of forever

we wouldn't have to heal over
and over the way we dip the bread

in blood before it clots.

Gate Shot

Quick squeeze the tempered nerve.
A dime's wrath dusts your palm.

I steal a spark from the spoon
to fuse constellations in the coral

fabric. Yeah—it's another a joyride
at the witching hour, a race through

arteries and toll roads so we don't
trail past our demons in the slipstream.

August crawls, we look twice, violet skies
I've tracked, I'm dialed, craving clouds

which means I'm craving you
flushed from the gate shot. There's no

edge worth wiping our feet on after
we saw the borealis and cut its ribbons,

surprised by what we won't exhume:
the unclaimed ashes on the changing

counter, the powder we are we use
to smudge our belligerent complexions

so the jukebox glow feels a more
flattering neon. You're always

chasing that one number to carry
us out the door, vandalized, blurred

in wet paint from the bathroom stall
wall because you know that tinge of baby

blue won't cover over the catalogues
of defeat that slips between our

interstates to the bottom barrel
where we point and shoot the moon-

roof breeze with red strings which
only blossom through our exit wounds.

Rabbit Ears

Down a service road. Postpartum
and cursing like the wind, like the
transistor on the bucket in my

father's shed that kept on always.
Static and beer. A wrenched
antenna. Every tool by a nail.

I could match the pitch
but not the frequency to where
I'm the one I've never heard of,

to trace the mirrored stars as
your variation on a theme and
ride the waves to radio silence.

When I was baptized in a bathtub
I froze the current to learn your
ripples, now my lungs don't burn

under water like they used to.
An ocean with no shore.
I became the gospel of bars

in every storm drain and still
to this day I can't dry off. I was holy
and I was pure as scripture, slack-jawed,

Novocain nods, drooling like a
gutter on the corner of Brevard
where I tried to talk to God through

a walkie-talkie with the same conviction
I had as a boy, trying to erase the darkness
with a flashlight. I was doped and heaven-

sent for last notes exhaled through a
harmonica, to lasso the 3am train before
the trumpet man fell breathless on the tracks.

Monarch

To cope with dusk, I vacuum flies from a chandelier,
from exit signs now that spiders only trap caterpillars

of light. They hoard the harvest. It's on the house
but not that way. We are sewn, cocooned in cobwebs

if the silk's too thin for the needle, a languid species of
pesticide. It bugs me. We get the wings we deserve,

pinned to a board, yellowed and archived in a drawer
underneath the register where I loved you from the

start, nocturnal, posed and wild as the ink-riddled
goodbye you sealed with your tongue. *Hello, darling,
I'm sorry.*

We were moth balls in a bowl of oranges. I tried to
spare the enigma's weave that couldn't permeate

the graffiti in my veins. In other words, the mirage
devours us whole, and again I miss your venom

kisses like I do the beads of amaretto puddling off
your neck as you'd tread my skin like a desert.

When do we evolve outside our exoskeletons?
To dodge nets and swatters blinding us with what we

don't realize we're missing once we're stunned again
by flames that lure us closer to the heated end.

Nevada Boulevard

Smoke glows brighter than an open wound
you cauterize with a cigarette. Odds are

the fountain coins will weigh you down.
And so as luck would have it, we are imprints

of carbon, perpetual jet lag, a consequence
of electric confetti rivaling the casino glare.

You were going to walk me through this,
how to erase this town in January rain,

but the sidewalks buckled and then the roads,
accordions of concrete like I was the ignition,

yelling wild numbers across the bingo hall
and couldn't stop until I won the rabbit's foot

buried in an ash tray. If it's all probability
then what's to prove? A high-rise skeleton

made of cards, helicopters low enough
you can almost catch their rope. I'm a byproduct

of fumbling desire should I pick the ace
of clubs up your sleeve or risk the joker's

fractured jaw. More or less alive, I call
off the cavalcades running out on nothing.

So what you pawn I will redeem, your sling-
shot for a golden bomb, I detonate like a sunset.

Mannequin Blue

Black frost. Silver thaw.
The light hesitates for its own good.
When airy pastures lead to crowded cliffs
an alarm clock stutters
off the nightstand, minutes all the same,
generations blink across the dotted wall-
paper like how did we get here?
She left the Tempo idling in Roswell.
Wipers waving to a cloudless sky.
So this is not a dream as it should be.
Though the ache is real, in lucid gloom,
a little groggy on the comedown.
But she comes back—steam hissing
like a factory stampede, ironing her
fists by the motel window. It's a tight rope.
Drenched in the overwhelm, she feels
for parallel stitches, unthreads miles
of twine from her knuckles, loosens
every last pin and flings them to a bowl.
She trips on the mannequin's train,
straddling a chair with its head spinning
round like a globe. She cuffs. She throws.
She tailors her spine, her pulse drums
louder than oceans uncorked to cover
tomorrow's ruins—to be seen in less
is to be hollow is to be true.

Violet moths. White amnesia.
A foghorn blares for sleepwalkers
as she drifts in a nightgown in a town
she can't pronounce, chasing her
mother's dress made of charcoal.
If we were formed by friction,
from ruts and scraping rocks,
then why aren't her cheeks sharp
enough to cut through boarded buildings?
But she doesn't know her way yet
with sparks, how stiletto earthquakes
can uproot a graveyard if the keeper's
on strike for more than a service, when
they fail to bait the traps on mausoleum
floors. The gate's wide open. She only
wears lipstick to funerals. A buried
phone rings from a robe for the whole
benediction. And she's reminded
of her contours, towels in the dryer,
the humdrum rumbling déjà vu,
the need to flatten geography,
how brief the geometry of a glacier.

Freezer Burn

I pull in late.
Ripe with the day's brine. Shuffle up the steps. Melodies of traffic like wannabe ballads still drumming in my ears, stale as the aimless motion, always rushing to this from that, always something as we go: a hole in a bag, tidal waves, rifling for keys in the other pocket. I set the groceries on the chair. Feed the fish. Water the plants. I kick a grape then eat it up off the rug. The cat's on the counter with her tail in the junk drawer left open. I scratch her back and ask her how she got here, who she thinks she is. But who am I? Craving salt as usual. Dinner's a warm beer and a fistful of olives, some pickles wrapped in Swiss cheese. You'd say that's not a meal. And I might agree. It's no mushroom risotto or peach pancakes after midnight, but I'm stuffed—like all those seasons we ate to kill the hunger pains, living in that closet above a laundromat with the slanted beams and spirits trapped in the radiator, our one and only window we could never close, could taste the cigarettes and bleach. All we had was that corduroy couch from the curb, blankets for a bed, no table to eat on but the piano bench to the old upright that came with the place. *Some things are too heavy to move,* the landlord said. *This will have to stay.* And it did. Because we didn't know how to be weightless with the surge that shook beneath, the 24-hour machines chugging away the grime like our legends, like the smoke alarm I busted with a broom after the cast iron biscuit incident, or the wishbone broth that simmered all winter long.

Together we learned, we listened to the impulse of getting by. Life was an inside joke.

Mornings we drank
government milk with cinnamon before setting out in our own directions. I'd try to sell my words to fit in perfect columns. I mean crumbs on the dollar. I'd write their threnodies for free. And you'd lug that cello from corner to corner, performing your sonatas next to a man stained gray who better identified as a statue. Sometimes an apple rolled into your case, a box of raisins, tangerine peels covering your music sheets. After the last applause you'd flatten a bill and hurry on to rummage through bruised produce in bins at the market doors: bananas, squash, plums, an onion, all the ugly skins, then pluck sprigs of mint and rosemary from a garden on North Brevard. I'd loiter at newsstands for the dirty talk or join a search party to get off the map for a while so I could stop and smell the oregano, pack my hands with basil and stems of thyme, a few tomatoes drooping over the barbed fence on Paradise Alley. Rarely are you found if you lead the way. The destinations always change. That or you're absorbed by the trees. What else. So it was habit I'd follow the same path back to South Elliot and scale the bottom shelf of the Minute Mart for dented cans and days-old bread, instant noodles, anything about to expire.

Sun down
we'd start again. Tired of the oatmeal sludge. We'd empty arms and tally the harvest, ration the stumps and rinds for stews to fill us through the weekends. If we had eggs and rice we'd fry it. You'd slice a carrot,

some broccoli. Cut around the brown. I'd dice a brick of spam and marry it all in oil. Shiitakes were a luxury. Chili filled us right. Peanut butter ramen was a lifeline to the mess we made, the accidents that defined our recipes, huddled in that hole of a kitchen, our backs pressed against each other, no one to be, water almost to a boil on a two-eyed stove, elbows nudging except for when we'd consider anyone who's died in a glimpse trying to get a closer view of the moon. *We fail to look both ways in a trance*, you'd say, grinding pepper into a sauce, crunching twigs of uncooked spaghetti while I'd shred lettuce or mash garlic into paste. We were lucky if we ate until we couldn't. Maybe whipped cream for dessert. A piece of mud pie where I'd eat the blueberry first and you'd save yours for the final bite, like the dishes piled to soak and clog the sink. Not enough soap in the world to strip the grease we leave behind. I'd pull sponges from the drain and scrub the bowls a thousand times as your fingers grazed the plank of piano keys, the muted notes and broken chords, and across the street the siren lights and song spilling through the curtain, swallowed by a galaxy of lint and foam.

    A bug flutters
in the blinds. The faucet leaks. And I am stuck like syrup charred to the bottom of a pan. How often do you lock yourself out now?—to walk in to cabinets wide open, the refrigerator's hum, all the magnets gradually to the ground. If you are not soaked or famished or both after the thaw, then what is it you still starve for? Thrills interrupted, when stability's an uneven table, a feast without an appetite. That's why the knives stay sharp, more than needed, Chinese on speed dial for those nights I botch another recipe from memory. Too

bland to be devoured. Too hot to taste a thing. The oven won't stop beeping as it's flush with an avalanche of crumbs on fire that smothers the lid to the sauce I stir and stir until it's steam and soon reduced so much you'd never know what it was before.

Push-Pull

Odd sounds. My charades. Blank walls
like picture noise. It's the rats, I'm sure,

revived from pharmacy post cards chewed
through a drop cloth. How do they still

fend for themselves? In an era, inaudible
so to speak, pressed for ribbons as dusky

voice overs loop and loosen off the tape.
You can't go back if you don't go forward.

Circles on the widow-walk. And here
I thought a jar of nails could keep

the door from swinging open. Just the
wrong side. See, I'm a dark smear

across your obscura. And I know you
know who haunts the shaken earth

when all the pipes are cold. Foreign
aromas like bells clashing. Mesmerized

by them. So don't pretend to ask what
crawls on moth floors unannounced,

bedridden as fires spread to the hollow
spaces of our polar opposites. Once, we

were parallel at arm's length. Vast yet not
enough. Reel to reel, skipping is as skipping was.

The Palm Reader's Son

Make it make sense, she said. Please.
        Drawn raspy and reaching.
     That feral feeling come dusk in disguise.

Here—my splints, vitals like faint luminosities,
        my wars, these hands hatched
     from gauze. Tell me what's too bright

to fathom, blinded by the fold, show me
        how to shine until I can't be seen,
     until I beg again for whatever's left in sight.

But you don't have the bones or the attention
        span to glue back together the glass
     splatter of a wild guess. And what's to say

otherwise after you watched a man drown
        through her shielded fingers?
     In the cold. A stone's throw. When

the dock dissolved into the bog. Who made
        you look? Cupped your ear,
     covered mouth. Ever since, double

takes in an Elvis chapel. Lady of the pines.
        I'm sorry I won't explain questions
     that answer themselves. And while

she sleeps, you wiggle on through the grove,
        this immediate moment,
   apparitions prancing around pits

in the ground so now we must find somewhere
        else to die. My liquid predictions
   ask for unspeakable toils blistered

in memory. And for every one, you pulled a
        splinter from your palm, hours after
   I lost your grip, blotting ants on the card table.

The Arsonist's Daughter

What will burn will burn because it can.
Not because it should. If seduction inspires
the first breath of a flame then whatever's
still left standing does not speak the language
of oxygen. So wrap yourself in wet sheets
and collect all the pieces that outlived
the glow of his orange desire, and barricade
yourself deep underneath the sediment.
Far from the lingers of his butane breath,
his magic and gasoline. Last winter he set
the lake on fire to resurrect the boiling point
of God in anyone held hostage by their former
selves. Except no one could afford the ransom.
I guess it's hard to barter with your reflection
knowing there are casualties on both sides.
The wind exhaled and sparks climbed
the trees higher than we ever could.
Empty bird nests flared like meteors
as dead leaves clenched into shrinking
fists that would never see revenge.
Before the canopy sank, he took off his coat
and draped curtains of smoke over his shoulders
and retreated into that cage of flames,
mired in the encore of his incineration.
        Your voice carried like emergency sirens
on back roads with no names, tangled in detours.
I was two wrong turns away from obscurity
before you showed me where the pavement ends,
and what the maps are hiding. No one asks for

directions anymore because all your shortcuts
lead to water. And that undertow you created
will send you drifting to places that know nothing
of home. So you built a raft from burnt matchsticks
and held on to the last one to preserve the novelty
of longing, to kiss the lips of the arsonist's
daughter where you learned the art of self
combustion. That's why everything I touch
leaves behind a permanent shadow, fooled again
by the shade for the warmth in the white noise
of a burning forest.

Hotel Eleven

I am an echo between two windows. My aura
distorted—ricocheting off the available chaos

since patterns bloomed like black umbrellas.
I wade through motion sickness to plug holes

in parentheses because I crave the algebra
of logical disasters that can't be outlined in chalk.

Eleven helicopters, counting. I churn a kaleidoscope,
watch my equations dissolve like chemical dreams.

That's why you're flipping pillows. The fan struggling
on low. I unzip my suitcase, pan for artifacts

and heartbeats as a knot of curtain cords shiver
in a blizzard of analog snow. If reruns are forever,

then how vacant must the highway hum
in order to calculate the temporality of home?

My erratic estimations. You were the air in a piano,
the inertia of a rented room. And here I am again

punching buttons to dead-end elevators until I am left
second-guessing the endlessness of a hotel hallway.

A paramedic performs open-heart surgery on a bench
in the lobby. You cross mine every once in a while

so when we collide you walk through me. You make
me want to float above myself and the cart that rolls

by with washcloths, clicking like a stuck revolver
because drooping from every door handle reads:
do not disturb

*do not resuscitate, do not disappear into the folds
of a trench coat*. But you were already a ghost

dancing on my back, lazy pirouettes, always
the same number, like a ballerina in a box.

Baggage Claim

Spit cracks the curb.
Iridescent blots. What puddles

like tongues sharpened mouth
to mouth, three stories not high

enough to feel the tailspins
of devastation. I chew the ice

melt from a bucket. Curate
the quiet moments, the dim

flicker of a cherry's flare, siphoning
gas from cars with broken headlights

when the impact's more trouble
than it's worth. Like swan songs

choked mid-sentence. Or letters
scrawled on coasters in airport bars,

reaching for anyone's suitcase
but my own I wheel around turn-

stiles of terminal delay. Dear first light
at the counter window, I don't know

where I'm coming from. But how
quick can you write me off the rocks?

Postmarked. Returned to sender.
The address hatchet-carved

to the stump in your field of vision
you'll never see even if you're squinting.

What We Can't Take with Us

I'm held up in a gift shop.
Broke as usual, leafing through bumper

stickers of all the things we'd rather drive
further away from ourselves. How far

is far enough to swerve and still regain
composure? I saw the ice and walked

across. I have no proof I was there.
However the man at the door clears

his throat and screams about a robbery,
and I guess for a minute I'm amused

when he questions what's so funny
and I point to the banner *Going out*

of Business like the empty shelves
of his mind. The cherubs are stocked

but not for sale. And yet we negotiate
with thieves as if we're late for lunch

and no one's laughing now at postcards
of Armageddon, like the one with your grainy

face above the register, blending in with
the mobs, a wooden angel piercing through

your bag and the keychain with another
spelling of your name looped around

your thumb. Tell me what it's like to feel
stranger than yourself, when it's time to go,

it's all on discount, and everything
but the rush is for taking.

Hang the Clothes to Dry

Quiet like pistol
to pillow talk of a clouded
memory you can't assemble even
if you wanted to: back watching

breaths, juice through a straw,
the washer's thrum and dryer
churning a dizzy child, flamingos
fading from his shirt since you've

grown so fond of bleach. The denim
vest doesn't fit, candy stripes to white
attire, we dilute the muddied stories
we prefer but won't explain the wear

like we were something spotless,
like hearts on sleeves too small that curl
from every flashback pinky promise
parted on a whim. We unravel

the seconds. Dyes bleed from the frays.
I smoke the light from every bulb
in every room, because how lifeless
a lifetime can be, falling in circles above

the well when it's dry. We toast an empty
auditorium, evacuate our ruins to get
locked out again, a polyester backdrop
to this nowhere reality I think I finally

know you only as a spin cycle crisis, if
at all, bound to chemistries and tragic
concoctions, our hundred parts watered
down and still too potent for soap.

Original Bliss

Thunder strikes a car alarm that isn't ours
but I'm suspicious. You know, the way

the light attacks mid creation. And
the slope we climb to steal back

our silhouette's been leveled
for a chop shop. But you take a number.

You're not a thief yet. Even despite
our borrowed parts. Blood still rushes

back to our limbs like storms before
we'd deconstruct our arid bodies

from chrome reflections
off faucet knobs and exhaust pipes.

If we could pawn the stupor of original
bliss, we would. When the plaster peeled

or burst. A string of drip buckets
from the stairs to the oven, to the shelf

by the door, gnawing on citrus rinds
as you sprayed vodka on the couch

to kill the must of ceiling water.
The fabric doesn't make a difference,

whatever drop cloths we're cut from,
you can't recover the sentimental debris
unless you crack your own safe first.

Cosmic Ray

His one suit hangs on your bedroom door
so you can take it to the funeral home

in the morning—a quick exchange, no desire,
take a mint from the urn on your way out.

The jacket was too big for his body, buttons
at the cuff sagging by some thread, why

he saved it from the basement flood you'll
never know. Tired but afraid to sleep now,

like he was, the wee hours he'd call along
a weary dialect, his voice like a tantrum

of engines, convincing you to stay awake,
to fight the night off with him, dragging

a shovel down the driveway even though
you know better than the darkness,

the drug it becomes once you pry the shine
from the blink of an eye. *Pain is open*

to interpretation, he'd say, but the buffet closes
at dawn, and we won't survive another relapse;

so you taper the seams and hem the sleeves,
pad the armor underneath, the way we dress

the dead after the metal's been mixed to look
like gold. He was hard to get a hold of.

Lens-locked. Camera shy, the only print of you
two together is blurry, otherwise life-like,

startled in a waiting room, which is every room
with a rack of magazines where he'd tear out

all the fragrance ads and rub his neck and cheeks
to smell like cabaret smog. Time is nothing when

it's all you have. Regular epiphanies, still influenced
by the hiss of speed, gut butterflies at the peak

until he'd crash-land in plain sight as you'd stand
there like a fortress worn with a smoker's cough.

He'd speak slow and hollow, brow dripping,
if the heavens are really above us, then all

the stars are yours to carry. From the switchblade
that carved us out the wall, back to original form,

just two darts in the middle of the ceiling.

Autumn Fog

It takes an algorithm to undress the solitude,
a thousand tiny earthquakes to shift the ink

in your still life. How many morning portraits
will you frame until the statue in the mirror

becomes more or less a smoke interruption?
Neon bleeds from your theories. Unusual beauty.

Tangible necessities. The whiskey missing
from the sink, where you forgot your features

as soon as the autumn fog enveloped you
like a mistress, even though—love is a train

exploding while we dance to a symphony
of sirens in reverse. I haven't stopped hoarding

jars of rain, still looking for scarce melodies
that made my eyes as bright as punch.

There's a saw screaming somewhere
in a forest. Tambourine death rattles.

I followed the blue railroad to hear her sing.

Helen

He loads film
to camera, checks his meter. Batteries. Checks again.
He eyes the map and folds, jams his pen, smokes and
compass, in that order, into a backpack, every morning
since the tremors turned to quakes. He zips the bag. He
leaves. A hug goodbye if you're on the chair. Notes on
the wallpaper when you're not. How close can you get
before the needle spins faster than itself? A hundred-
some years of sleep and now she's gnawing at the brink
of plates and floral decipherings, like the yellow
blossom era—everyone together in front of the wagon,
early July, picnic stills caged in Ponderosas. Mom and
dad had finally lost their words, staring past each other
while he balanced on the hood, looking at you atop a
boulder, twirling a limb twice your size that nearly
shattered the windshield when it fell.

Almost twenty miles
to the base. He blinks. Shifts to fourth. She floods the
distance again as if the first time, his first photo of the
summit towering above the trees, a jagged speck from
the driveway. Eventually you forget it's there at all. A
cigarette between the lips unlit. The too-hot coffee now
cold. He arrives and parks before the barriers convene.
Gravel shivers on the road. But the path still remains.
He collects his angles. Zooms in—up. Documents the
steam, the crater through the ice cap, an arctic haze of
ash and snow. And once out of rolls, he rewinds the day
under red light in a bathroom he used to share with his
brother who jacked a Harley for some dust, changed his
name to Bear and disappeared to the desert. The bike

was moss green. Pipes louder than alley backfires. Then the walls. The carpet. And still he burns vignettes of her ascent so dark it saturates the grain. But whose perspective? Contours bloom in chemical troughs. A whole mountain-side spilling from the tub.

Each night he stirs
a little more after the fan shakes off the dresser. With it his watch. Matches. An empty bottle or a dull blade. It's hard to dream while you push and pull the furniture around the rooms as if they ever fit from the start, gasping like curtains caught in a vacuum. The couch is flush with the hall again for the third time this week. Charcoal-smothered blue. The mantle missing the double exposure of you within yourself at the bottom of a canyon that once was a sea. He doesn't ask. You couldn't tell him why. Nor can he explain the ribbon hoards of half-framed negatives smeared in light-leak curling off the shower rod. How many faces eclipsed by flares? Vacant sceneries, pitch black terrains. The one of him and part of you braced against a constant sky, wind-breakers, just your arm wrapped around his sleeve.

Ten-thousand earthquakes
as of May. Nothing left on the shelves but crumbs and clouded peaks. He reassembles his things. Cuts his thumb—lens cracked and out of focus, secures something wider. You're nowhere in sight. Evacuation routes serpentine from the 5-0-4 outside his peripheral. As the crater deepens, he takes the same pictures at the same places. New vents. Sulfur in the air overrides the pine. The dome swelling now beyond her form.

He calls the day, finds a clearing for a tent and all night listens to her breathe like lone explosions. And late the next morning, he wakes to landslides, the ground shivering like God sifting for gold. He knots his boots. Unties his stomach. Points his camera at her crown as it detonates strata miles into the sky and all he can do with minutes to spare is shoot as fast as he can to fill the frames with what he can't believe and buries his camera into the bag and hugs it to his chest and sinks on himself but is carried back in ash before he even hits the ground.

Pretty Lush

Couple drinks. Couple lies
to convince yourself

this disguise is picture perfect.
A mask to cover pores,

my mistakes like tenants
in your thoughts with eviction

notes plastered on doors
because who can afford the rent

at these depths.
We imitate. We justify

our habits. We compose apologies
with weighted limbs as splinters

turn to daggers when a couple
drinks the silence and breaks

the bar: he's a rag-doll she mops
her dreams with, detaches in a

blink, but she haunts him, slurs so
after a couple lies next to one another

like nests in a gutter.

Giants

We were giants in a dollhouse,
microscopic moths
tapping on the glass from inside
a snow globe. We toasted to the monks

in the fridge. Then they clipped our
wings and left us to unstitch the noise.
The dreams were liquid, they were cold
and heavy, they were ours to invade.

We rode the avalanche down the stairs
and moved like fluid silhouettes through
the hallway. Just a slow parade of single
cells caught in the afterglow of time.

I was inanimate. We were marbles
rolling back and forth in a drawer.
Generations colliding, the trees bending
sideways are the reasons why I never

write about flowers. It was a rebellion
of the senses: depleted dopamine silos,
drained the serotonin reservoirs
because we couldn't ration the euphoria.

But we found the universe's alias
in the fabric of a napkin. We became
the patterns inherited by the light.
We learned we were gray.

Migratory Patterns

He hovers above the sink like an old disease.
Half-chewed noodles soak in sponge water.
The soup's been on the stove for a week.
He runs the faucet cold, waits for rust to stir
lily pads of olive oil, and feeds a coil of bruised
apple skin to the drain. *If I were an orchard*,
he says, *I'd be barren*, like branches in barbed wire,
pinches a wet cigarette and slides the seeds
into a matchbox.

Memories degrade the way a stray dog paces
along living room walls until the floor fades
to sawdust. The foundation sinks like a stomach.
And he is starved like a scarecrow, flinching
at soft ground, still carrying the limp of his father.
But when the creek dries in spring he lets the coyotes
eat from his hands, listens to them breathe
like a cello wheezing in rehearsal.

When the flood returns in fall he rearranges
the mantle with ceramic birds. He keeps a robin in his
pocket, splinters in his shoe. There were mourning
doves and orioles, a flock of wrens and a blue jay, a
few sparrows too. Glue drips from a gun onto beak
and wing, creates new species from feathers he's saved
from every foreign constellation that's been brushed
into a dustpan. So stiff and delicate, another vague
Madonna, the way he shatters into an echo of his own.

Weather Reports

You're in a diner in the middle of nowhere
you've never been, nude as the night,

pouring sugar into coffee because you hate
the taste of metal. You sit at the counter,

unroll silver, push the spoon to the side
like the one you love. The TV's on. Tornado

sirens, and the man caught in the spitting
rain is not impressed by your regrets.

Could have or should have but didn't and won't.
He drags his finger across time

and frames everyone to look like someone else.
But you know better than the camera's blur, the way

he spins around and breathes into the microphone—
I thought the sky only collapsed in rearview mirrors.

You have to retrace your geography for a storm
worth believing. And soon it's egg shells

on blistered linoleum. A peninsula of abandoned cars.
We all think it's a test but it's not. The waitress

clicks her pen. Stampede amnesia. You didn't order
an omelet with toast, but you eat it anyway.

Compass Rose

You're tracing wires with your eyes.
Landlocked. The invariable nod of your finger
roping off the tree line. You can blink out here
and not miss a thing. You can drive
long enough until you feel like a ship in a bottle
rolling in place at the end of a conveyor belt.
You can stare. Or you can separate shadows
from your vanishing point and swallow the distance
before it begs you to switch lanes. But slow to recoil
your tunnel vision narrows out of habit. Breadcrumbs
intersect with detours and shoulders you traded
for rain checks. How the engine drones on like an
argument, ribs aching for Roanoke. Heat leaks
through a cracked windshield as a neon flyer slips
from the visor onto the dashboard, promising two-
hundred miles to the sea. The captain calls—an SOS.
Cuts the anchor like a poem. Says he's an expert in
capsizing but never learned how to float. Maybe what
lies beyond a bleach-stained horizon gets taken back
by the undertow. Except for the moon, which always
sways from the rearview like a dream catcher,
cobwebs and already you're expired once you feel
brand new. There was a forest of pine fresheners in
the glove compartment, the last one wedged in the
vent points north. On your way, if you pass the boy in
a hospital gown selling painted roses from a bucket on
the over-pass, fill his cup with quarters and he'll pile
the back seat with as many bouquets tied in
tourniquet bows— so wherever it is you go, hugging
the road, far from your exits, you can surround your
empty spaces with thorns as real as love.

Inkwells

Dream leave.
Chase or be chased or

pull the attic string
like a piano on a crane.

Hammers hit the ladder
slides one foot off the pedal.

There's a stroller on the road,
and you're skipping stairs

with legs too heavy to lift
above the charge, so you fall

flat as old songs from the big red
book where a boy stands on top

to touch the keys, to press the notes
that hurt our ears, a chorus of

peppered throats in the backseat
neon spaces of your mind. How

do you get out of your way, when
it's so loud, no matter where we are

anymore, no sustain for the man
in the tunnel preaching to rails

from a microphone plugged in
to nothing. I'm broke but it's not

your fault. And what doesn't croon
gets me every time. A stampedes

ephemera. Lipstick smears on
a shop-keep window, delirium

scribbles in bullet light.

Arrowheads

I think I thought I saw an arrow
break your gaze. A murmur
from the margins, the static child
by a sling, arrested then released,
like a cannon ball through the cabin wall.
I guess it lets the light in unannounced,
no shine but a glimmer, you know, like it
were here to stay, but it's not and you're
convinced, so you thought I heard the air
raids from the meadow. First a crackle
then a burst—we were thunderstruck
junkies and at it again, as if we could
still be shaken, but I was on a hill and
you were blowing fog into the mirror
for that spitting image, the one with
war paint flaking off your every exhale
after you slalomed through dive
bombs and angels dusting for easy targets,
trying to look half alive, which is half
the battle really, the way your holster rides
off your leg once you're down to your fighting
weight. All those notches in your belt,
nicks in your skin, and the more you shed
the more you swung into craters padded
by heaps of nests fallen, rallying cries
out of reach and marching on through
clover while I pushed blanks to the chamber
of your secret weapon. Even with a head
start you stood back into the volleys, the blind

spots we used to outrun before the debris
eclipsed our accumulations like train cars
connecting for the long haul. Where to though,
and what now of the burden with one left
in the quiver and a second wind when we
still haven't seen the Sierras but for the bear
he lugged home and flattened to the floor
we weren't allowed to cross, its snout aimed
at the musket above the mantel held heavier
than legend of the beast I keep unloading
since you can't get passed the wreckage
if you audit the shrapnel.

Vanishing Point

We dug our heels in the sand.
Pelicans mobbed the surf for chum.

A driftwood barge combed the horizon.
Caked in salt. New year. We hadn't said

a word past Reno. Another bridge torched
behind us for the hell of it. Yet there we

were. Washed up. Wrapped your arms
around your jagged knees and nursed

this paradise to a lonesome pulp.
From what it was, precarious love.

The sum of anchors lost and tongue-
tied seductions, the way you'd pinch

a jay to my lips from over your shoulder,
how I'd lean in for a drag and hold until

the tide retreated. Right away, I'd sink
into you, like a battering ram, punctuate

the melancholy to drown out the archives
of bloom and sorrow. We were warned.

Can't get the wind back once it's been
knocked out of us. We furled the shadowed

sails too soon. If the point is to capsize,
then how much longer till we're rounded

by the sea? *Any minute now*, you said,
yesterday, no, was a decade ago.

NOTES

Giants is for Peter Brown

Cosmic Ray is for Trenda and Ray Boone

Helen is loosely inspired by the only three surviving photographs Robert Landsburg took on May 18, 1980 of the Mount Saint Helens eruption. He was a *National Geographic* photographer documenting the activity for a few months. He was seven miles from the summit the morning it blew.

ACKNOWLEDGMENTS

I'd like to express my sincere gratitude to the editors of the following magazines and journals, where some of these poems first appeared.

Appalachian Review
Mannequin Blue, Subdivisions

Asheville Poetry Review
Hotel Eleven

Broken Tribe Review
Knotted Wave

Crosswinds Poetry Journal
Tea Leaves

great weather for MEDIA
Migratory Patterns

Iodine Poetry Journal
Autumn Fog

Jabberwock Review
Bridled, What We Can't Take With Us

Jet Fuel Review
Circuits

Kakalak
Giants

Lily Poetry Review
Weather Reports

Main Street Rag
The Arsonist's Daughter

The Midwest Quarterly
Understanding Gravity, Nevada Boulevard

New York Quarterly
The Palm Reader's Son

Pedestal Magazine
Freezer Burn, Vanishing Point

ABOUT THE AUTHOR

Chad Weeden's poems have appeared in *The Midwest Quarterly, Pedestal Magazine, Jabberwock Review, The Asheville Poetry Review*, and elsewhere. He is a portrait photographer and lives in Rhode Island. For more information, please visit chadweedenphoto.com.